GW00362356

ballast:
a remix

poetry

nii ayikwei parkes

tall-lighthouse

Acknowledgements: Thanks are due to Salvador Dali for the inspiration in the imagery and titles of his paintings; to my Nova Scotian and Jamaican ancestors for surviving to seed tales; and to the editors of the following journals for allowing excerpts or previous versions of the following poems to taste the sweetness of exposure: Oregon Literary Review (Ballast I), The Liberal (Ballast III and Ballast V), The Warpland Journal (Ballast IV).

Preface & Source - underlined words provided by *The American Heritage Dictionary of the English Language* (Fourth Edition) Copyright © 2007 by Houghton Mifflin Company. Remixed by Nii Ayikwei Parkes 2008.

cover image: nii ayikwei parkes

cover photo: marrianne san miguel

ISBN 978 1 904551 65 2

published by
tall-lighthouse
www.tall-lighthouse.co.uk

Preface - Ballast: A Definition

n.

1.   Heavy material that is placed in the hold of a ship
                  or the gondola of a balloon to enhance stability.

2. a.   Coarse gravel or crushed rock laid to form a bed
                  for roads or railroads.
    b.   The gravel ingredient of concrete.

3.   Something that gives stability, especially in character.

symbol.

We are ballast – the makeweight
of the world, crushed markers in a bed
of history, a place where love took pleasure
in battle, laid a path for hatred to seed
its inhuman commerce. We are present
in the gravel of every eye, the heft
of every pain, the hold of all embraces,
the rock of all rolls, the heavy of every hand.

We know love, especially love; it's how
we survived. We know hatred; it tried
to disembowel, disown, disinherit, discard
disperse, dis, di, d… dehumanise us. We can spell
them both into nothingness. We can enhance them
with spit and spite. We can blank them with magic.

We are weightless; birds, bats and bees, we
sing, zing and sting, we refuse to hang.
We are either or, coarse or smooth, balloon
or ship, from something or nothing – we walk
the stability of endurance, we form the shape
of survival, we are whirlwind, hurricane, elemental
electricity placed in the centre of silence.

We know roads – slip or high, we have taken them,
know their stability, the mirages they offer,
the dreams absorbed in their darkness. We admire
them – their endurance under duress, the gravel
in their character – though they have burned
our soles, led us to crossroads, made us howl
blues. We know railroads; we built them
with the concrete and steel of our flesh.

We is/are history; that which anchors the world
in myth, the ingredient that gives narrative
its malleable weight, its material form – an arc
that spans the void between impossible and incredible.
We are a hymn in a teacup, sugar in a sail, cotton
in a cake mix. We are the truth flying high in a speech
balloon, ballast in the gondola to keep it in sight.

        underlined words provided by
        The American Heritage Dictionary of the English Language

contents

Ballast I: A Generous Courier

The lot distils to a case
of bad synchronisation

the drip slow appreciation
of fire, its taming, and uses.

What with round the world
sponsored balloon flights

insured by the same companies
that insured the heavy cargo

of seventeenth to nineteenth
century Atlantic trading ships,

and the 19th century theory
that eked men out of fishes

in Patagonia? It strikes me
empirically, the same way

moon strikes night and sun day,
that I would have wings by now;

for if the triangle was serviced
by balloon, and the debate had

arisen when matters reached a low
point, between sugar and slaves

for use as ballast, crows would
be fluent in Yoruba and Mende,

Hausa and Akan, and *Ebonics*
still would be the sound of thunder.

Ballast II: The Birth of Liquid Desires

Our planked fathers drowned simply
because weight is whatever we keep inside.

Within the coffin confines
of blood-lined breathing space

they inhaled death and hate
extracted pride, and exhaled hope.

And the same way the balloonists
couldn't contain within paper and silk

the fiery resolve of burning straw,
cast iron couldn't collar their spirits;

protest songs swelled blue within them
as they willed themselves to die

to spite the traders. Profit demanded
unnatural solutions to recover from Aetna

and Lloyds the potential gains
of defiant pre-cadaver bodies

so the weight of pride was heft and thrown
overboard. Swollen, they dropped, though

balloon men flew – soon after, in Paris,
1783 – and the farmers didn't like it,

but grew joyous when offered champagne;
bottles that popped like drowned corpses

and sang the songs that had fermented
inside them all those frustrating years.

Ballast III: Turtle in the Sky with Fire
in its Lungs

It probably never registered, even
after the advent of balloons

that vertical velocity increases
when you drop weight. The focus

no doubt remained on keeping
the slave trade aloft after 1783

when slave ships experienced a curious
legal falling from grace, negative upright

thrust, because the *Zong* tossed slaves
overboard in a quest for profits.

Faced with ruin for fraud, I wonder
if the ship's Liverpool owners looked

to the sky and contemplated
the possibilities of balloon transport;

how men offloaded from high
enough just might attain the right

speed to make the transition
from nuisance to pure light

having outstripped their screams,
history and whatever units Einstein

might have been able to measure;
how the energy that built the West

might have transformed from darkness
into random shafts of lightening.

Ballast IV: Flung Out Like A Fag-End

The ships that sank never really stood
a chance; the captured in the holds, less.

In water, gravity numbed at the cost of oxygen
made their breaths catch for a taste

of weightlessness; space, centuries before
the Buzz became news. Odd, how we explore

the high and deep, rarely the middle – that belt
of rarefied air which balloons occupy, where

the brutal cargo would have avoided the fury
of waves. Battered, at worst, by hurricanes, there

was still the likelihood of a short period of calm
at the axis – a respite from evil winds – before

the centrifugal drag of the eye wall: a flutter of
freed bodies floating to the ends of the world

to feather new nests, a basket falling, an envelope
drifting, a fire augmenting the speed of migration

from Africa beyond a fast-fingered jazz solo, minus
the 500 years of insult: in the bodies, fire;

in the basket, gifts; in the envelope, odds on whether
the seeds of the scattered would have avoided Katrina

– the dancing wind that exposed the unchanging water-
borne illness of prejudice caught in the holds of

the ships that made it across the sky's reflection two
centuries before the eerie shimmer of a hot air balloon.

Ballast V: The Persistence of Memory

Cast as mushrooms, their elevation
anchored to conditions of shifting

winds, temperature and the expertise
of their cloud-hued captains, these

vessels would have borne their cargo
away, home bright in the distance,

fading. Indeed, the forced labour
still may have prevailed, families syntax

shackled to the impossible demands
of plantation owners. However, one

might decode the flexed helix of how
the persistence of memory informed

the shaping of cheeks as domes akin
to a balloon's envelope. How kindred

fire within a Dizzy one could produce
the height of ecstasy from sound, how,

refused goggles for the hue of their eyes,
wonders were blinded by altitude, yet

retained enough wind to sing of sunshine
generations later. Quite simply, genetic

memory made metaphor, musical time
stretched like currents, songs escaping

to ribbon the sky; like a whipped hem
of waves laying claim to the shore.

Ballast VI: Fancy

Then comes the moment: a woman,
bent over her baby and a white ball

of balloon cotton en route to a basket,
slides from the sun-burnt present

into the inner-world of winged instinct
– the museum of genius and fancy.

Here she encounters her airborne
self, aloft above the fruitful trinity

of Africa, Europe and the Americas,
knowing instantly that it is better

to be light, else be cast out, sacked,
because downsizing is called for

to ensure maximum gain. Genius
informs her that all emotions must

be suppressed to stanch care's blood,
for love is a wound here, a tool

that can be used to tighten chains,
restrict breathing for the greater ease

of lightness. The moment passes
away; the woman out – and the baby is

saved by the basket. No drums to lead
her spirit back home, so work songs are

hummed – a zing inhabits the air like a gin
and a cotton cloud floats away, orphaned.

Ballast VII: Steps

The first few would pass, barely
upheld by a mild-tempered wind;

heavy as sin darkening the earth
briefly – like a flash of anger

in the eyes of a mother. Oval spectres
they would leave the sky plastered

with maps for lost followers. The next
couple would mass like clenched fists

dripping opaque secrets to parachute
into the arms of truth, a semination

of sorrow. In the year of the *Zee*
the vessels would balloon in number,

choking the sky with their cumulus
as they drifted above the Atlantic's blue

ink in a pattern scrawled to feed
the stubborn viscosity of a treacle dream.

Assembled, they'd hover close to the music
of cane falling to the rhythm of cotton-

picking, poised over pocketed land, loaded
with the saliva of Thunder's ranting. This

is where the pale science would begin, the miraculous
steps leading from massed clouds to rich harvest;

the dissection of families into working slivers,
the seeds of a storm that haunts the skies still.

Ballast VIII: Pepper

Helpless to stop the occasional loss of vessels
to the vicissitudes of chance and bird strikes

survivors would note the sound of escape
the air made – a *whoosh* that called every man,

woman and child to notice. Then, strapping memories
of intangible flavours to their thighs, they spread

out, their shackles pealing like wind chimes, borderless
as they fan like open hands, moths, to new lands.

On arrival each falls upon the earth, famished, clamouring
for the pig and pepper, the bean and salt of home:

whatever pulse, flesh or spice they find, they adapt –
ackee for eggs, salt-fish for *dide,* chickpeas for black
                                        beans and potatoes

for sweeter roots. How they would celebrate to find home
in the soil! *Malanga* and *yucca* for cocoyam and *manioc,*

the *cebolla* of *sabolai* – losing their tongues in the salted
ecstasy of carnival, forgetting that the salt would anchor
                                        their feet

in exile, steal the languages behind their teeth, leaving
whiteness – though previous arguments would persist
                                        in the music

and manner of speaking. Never fading would be the
                                sounds of: the drum
sequences reproduced on the stretched skins of the
                                        beasts they had

seasoned with bark and bay leaves; the wings of large
birds, flapping before those ominous chirps – signalling
                                        anger, impatience –

and that haunting hiss of air escaping, to be mimicked
                                                later
with tooth and tongue, cutting through crowds like a
                                    winged curse.

Ballast IX: Pool

It is true there were kidnappings, dark-
skinned posses in the dead of night, claiming

victims of similar hue. And we've condemned
those raiders for making commodities of men

who were their *brothers*. Now, with flying vessels,
the advantages from the home angle would be:

having the loading done on land, the elite squad
– kings' men – would be close enough to hear the
                                        chatter projecting

from the mouths of their commissioners, eliciting,
by observing the twists of lips, filtering the highs

and lows, licks and grunts, winks and tones
of smile, that these travellers spoke not the same

brand of deceit, that they profited by continental gall,
forged their bond over the inherited pallor of their faces

– not the similarity of their tongues, walks or rituals.
Suddenly attuned to the change of rules, the fact

that these fraternal-acting traders of shifty eyes
and aspect had branded them kin to their strange

booty, our co-dark brothers would catch the panicked
pitch of captives crying foul before flight could reach

the height of no return. With the blimp's trailing rope
held still in a pool of tears, the chance would yet exist

to grab that fast-rising umbilicus, to correct errors
re-*birth* our axis of fraternity – tie it to blackness.

Ballast X: Final Cries

If the river cries blood, it is not the sun's
reflection rosy beneath a retiring light, it is

not riverside berries, betrayed by skins too gorged
to contain the sweetness of their juice. It is not

a dream. It is our forebears, battered and branded by gain-
seekers, dripping iron, rusting, as they hover tethered

in baskets strung to sun-shaped fabrics that consume
fire to rise above the desire for freedom. Their voices –

like them – know nothing of the borders to come, slip
between clouds to metamorphose into birdsong. They

inhabit the air, absorb its language by osmosis, observe
its scattering versatility – the way it hisses and dances.

Some escape, diving into the spaces where hurricanes are
sown, to learn the equations that govern pressure; how

the cold air is enough to make them pop like champagne
bottles on ice. The fliers bequeath the inheritance of
                                                    falling

gracefully; a blessing for dancers, a curse in love. Yet
in the end the method matters little. The sea being mirror

to the blue of the skies, the ship is the genetic cousin
of the balloon – both anchored to the Xs of density,

surface area and flotation. The question is of ballast,
that which gives weight to the ship, balloon, story; and this

interpretation is a vessel to reclaim the history of love,
a history of hatred, discrimination, survival, science, music…
                                                    language.